D1085842

The Cynic's Guide to Being Happy

Randall W. Dunkle

DEDICATION

To my parents. Thanks for raising me the only way I could have
been raised. And to happy cynics everywhere.

CONTENTS

INTRODUCTION

There are many reasons why you may be reading this book. Maybe you felt connected to the title. Maybe you passed it in the bargain bin and your spouse is taking too long in the store next to the book store. Maybe you feel you are just cynical enough to enjoy the treasure trove of good advice, anecdotes and life lessons printed on these pages. Most likely, if you are like the millions of other readers out there, you liked the way the jacket looked. The particular font called out to you like a little typographic siren beckoning you to open the back cover and skim through the liner notes. Fine, whatever, as long as you bought the book.

Whatever reason you have for embarking on your new cynical yet happy lifestyle, rest assured, this book can help. The cynical life is not an easy one. It is a life of no expectations. It is a life of self discovery (and then, sometimes, self loathing.) A true cynic can't help but notice when he or she has completely humiliated his or herself. A true cynic also realizes that it won't be long until everyone around him or her does the same thing. We are all bumbling morons. Every jerk stumbling around on this floating rock is doing just that...stumbling. The most confident bastard you know has, at one time or another, gone home and cried himself to sleep because someone somewhere didn't love him, didn't choose him, or just plain didn't notice him.

At many times this book will seem like a contradiction. You may laugh during some passages, cry during others, and, during the more anecdotal passages, you may find yourself judging me. That's OK. We all do it. Be careful, though. These anecdotes were printed here; because, to be ashamed of them would be to pretend everyone hasn't been in a position of great humility or even humiliation. This is the greatest of untruths. See above statement regarding all of us being morons. The following chapters will be presented from a single point of view. I (Randy) am gay. Am I covering all possible bases? No. Why? Because, the only truly universal thing about human beings is that they all, at one point or another, have acted like an asshole. So, I cover a lot of that stuff in here.

That having been said, many of the following passages deal with people that infuriate me. Let us not forget, this book is about cynicism. There are people walking this earth that make me want to rip the very hair from my very scalp. But then I think, "Why not rip their hair out instead?" I digress. One might be apprehensive about labeling oneself a cynic. But, what I had to realize is while many people of this world irritate me beyond compare, I am no longer ever surprised by it.

There is a threshold within each of us, a membrane being pushed upon by the every day annoyances, moronic people, badly managed businesses and just plain bad luck. On the other side of this precipice is complete insanity. You aren't alone. Don't allow yourself to be pushed over the line. Dig in your heals, accept it, and expect nothing less. Consider this book your survival guide. Welcome fellow cynic. We've been waiting for you (but, we really didn't think you were going to show up).

Chapter 1

"Expectations are the seeds of disappointment."

Truer words have never been spoken. To me, there are few more infuriating things than disappointment. I want something to happen. It doesn't happen. I get really angry. Nothing continues to happen. Rinse and repeat.

Disappointment can come in many shapes and sizes. It can loudly announce its entrance with a great deal of fanfare or sneak up silently behind you and wipe a booger on your shoulder. It can happen anywhere. It can happen at work, at home, on the road, with friends, with boyfriends, with potential boyfriends, with pets, with movies, with television shows, you name it and you can probably be disappointed by it. Disappointment is a nasty tempered little bitch and will cut you down before you ever see her coming. Well, isn't that the very point. Disappointment has to have some form of transportation to reach you. Disappointment's favorite mode of transportation is the expectation.

Expectations are the Indian food that smells really good and disappointment is the moment you eat it and it tastes like a toilet. But what if you went into that restaurant thinking that the food probably wouldn't be that good? You just slashed the disappointment fairy's tires. She had no way of getting to you and wiping her butt with your dining experience. Some people might say, "Shouldn't we just have no expectations? Why go all the way to being negative?" These people are annoying. No expectations, bad expectations, whatever the case may be, just don't expect good things. Either one works. However, I have always found saying, "Just have no expectations." very similar to saying, "Just clear your mind." Can anyone really clear their mind? I have never been able to do this. The best I can do is just think of something stupid and innocuous. It is by this logic I recommend bad expectations. Because, we all know there will be some expectation. Just make sure they err on the negative side. This eloquently stated principle can be applied everywhere.

Disappointment at work, we have all experienced it. Here is the thing. Just accept it. No one is going to do their job. If you are good at something, every other slack hole around you will sit back and let your work ethic carry the load. This is life. People are lazy. They suck and they don't want to do anything. Expect them to do nothing and not only will you not be disappointed, but, you might be surprised every month or so when they throw you a bone and take a couple calls. (Or fast food orders. I am not sure what the demographic for this book is going to be.)

Movies and TV...Christ! I am not sure how to even begin. There are so many ways movies and TV can disappoint it is almost not possible to even write about it without the tears in my eyes blurring my vision. It doesn't seem like rocket science to me. If you watched your own movie and fell asleep, most likely other people are going to find it boring. If you cast your wife whose only previous work had been a couple guest spots on The New Fantasy Island, your movie is probably really bad. If it's based on a video game and "faithful" to that video game, your movie definitely sucks. TV producers can follow this same advice but with one added note. Treat your audiences like they are stupid and your show will not be smart. But, this brings up a good point. When I tune into a pilot, I fully expect it to be filmed trash. The main characters will be one dimensional assholes that bring every problem upon themselves and resolve them with deus ex machina that would make an ancient Greek playwright change the channel. If I find myself enjoying the show, my lowered expectations have saved me from a night of reading. I hate to read.

Relationships are going to be heavily examined in this book. The reason being, is there one sad bastard out there reading this that hasn't come home to your pet after a date and thought, "What if I just try being of a different sexual orientation?" People are the grandest farmers of the disappointment fruit and when romantic feelings are involved, the acreage of that farm just triples. It's a fact...or a metaphor. I haven't really thought it through. The short and skinny of it is, people have no idea what the hell they are doing when it comes to matters of the heart (or the genitals). At this point, even the most intelligent people may as well just strap on the helmet and wave down the short bus. The sad truth is, people are the only animal capable of analyzing love, lust, loss, rejection and all the other wonderful binge-drink-session worthy aspects to romantic interaction. The inherently instinctual drive to couple up mixed with the evolved sense of analytical obligation combine to form a shit storm the likes of which have ruined entire civilizations. The problem here is that most people, in some way, disappoint themselves at the same time they are disappointing you and then they can't differentiate whether you brought it out in them or if they just suck at everything. And, human nature being what it is, they inevitably decide that thinking about it requires too much time walking the tightrope of responsibility and they just blame it on you and stop returning your texts.

The key here is to expect everyone to be awful. In other scenarios you might be able to get away with not having expectations (if you believe in that fairytale), but here, we all expect something and when the disappointment doesn't come, it can really feel like you have won the lottery and you better not lose that fucking ticket. This is what leads to over-communication after one date and frequently the worst kind of disappointment. The disappointment cloaked by a pleasant surprise. This is the kind of disappointment to which cynics are most vulnerable.

Lesson 1:

It isn't the pessimistic person who evolves into a cynic. It's the optimistic person who developed a sense of realism. The world is a rough place; but, hidden throughout are wonderful people and funny situations that someday you can put into a book.

As I sit here, ready to move on to my next chapter but unable to think of a good transition, I think I will take the road of a true cynic and force a segue where there isn't one. I will take the laziest road and bring up stupidity out of nowhere in order to transition.

I have never been very good at segues or transitions. My mind works in a whirlwind of random thoughts held together by the weakest of connectors. I frequently switch subject in the middle of a conversation. I don't notice it. My mind made the connection somewhere and I went with it. This will be the only appropriate segue in the entire book.

Chapter 2
Part 1:

"The other 99%."

I have encountered a great deal of stupidity in my life. It's my cross to bear. Some people survive cancer. Some have an invalid child they must take care of. Some people have the arduous task of caring for a loved one with Alzheimer's. Me? I encounter the dumbest people on the face of the earth every single day. A proverbial revolving door of assholes seems to cyclone its way through my life on a moment to moment basis. Now I use the revolving door analogy because many of them are the same assholes that keep resurfacing. Over and over again they wander up to me, attempt to either lie to me, get me to validate some racist comment, fain apathy when I know they are dying inside or just to tell me a story about what some chick said on the phone while they were performing their job. You all know who you are. I say you know who you are because I would hate for people whom I have no problem with to misinterpret this passage.

You may notice over the course of this literary journey that I complain a great deal about stupidity. Consider this my cause. As getting dictatorships and atrocities media attention is for George Clooney or adopting several black children is to Angelina Jolie, I would like to abolish stupidity, or just get it as far away from me as possible.

The specific kind of stupidity I would like to discuss this evening, kids, is emotional stupidity. Yes, there is such a thing. Allow me to elaborate. Emotional stupidity is not having the intelligence to sort through your feelings and determine which ones are rational and should be expressed and which ones are irrational and shouldn't be allowed to be burdens to other people.

I am a believer in the theory that approximately 99% of the entire world's population is unrepentantly stupid. Actually, I am the progenitor of that theory; but, I digress. Think about it. 99% of everyone you encounter is a moron. And then there is that 1%, the happy few with whom you choose to spend your time, family, friends and the like. The other side of that worthless coin is that without the expectation of anything more, the disappointment brought upon by the revelation of a person's burdening stupidity is often avoided

Lesson 2:

This may seem like a cynical and pessimistic thought process. It absolutely is. But, not all of them need be. The fact is, every once in a while, everyone can start to feel like they are swimming upstream. The true cynic wallows in this feeling for a little while and then says, "Screw this.", gets out of the stream and starts walking uphill. Additionally, it helps to make those that reside in the 1% with you know they are appreciated.

However, I must admit that I find myself feeling jealous of those living this blissfully ignorant existence. Speaking of jealousy...

Part 2:

"Jealousy and other stupid emotions that stupid people will try to blame you for."

Now I am not saying that emotions are ever rational; but, emotionally intelligent people have irrational feelings every day. They examine and say to themselves, "This comes from my own insecurity. I should determine the source but not run and tell the person just because they happened to be around when I felt this." In contrast, emotional retards would have an inner monologue that would sound like, "I feel jealous. I feel angry because I'm jealous of Randy. Randy needs to hear how angry he has made me. He needs to fix it."

See what happened there? A completely legitimate yet irrational feeling was allowed to become a burden for someone who simply is living their life and not fucking up. Jealousy is just one symptom of emotional fuckupery; but, it's the most prevalent; therefore, I will be using it as an example for the remainder of the exercise.

If I were to feel jealous (everyone does from time to time), I would never want to tell the person of whom I was jealous about it. I would never want to make them feel bad for what they have earned, or even try to do so. More likely than not, the feeling is coming from me having a particularly insecure day or something else equally unimportant. More likely than that, they would just think me stupid for not going out and getting my own. Which is exactly what jealousy ultimately inspires me to do....act! It inspires emotional dumbasses to have a stupid conversation. See the difference? If you don't, it all comes down to a simple concept. You could read 100 books a day. You could have 3 degrees and own a successful medical practice. You could have a vocabulary consisting of the highest number of polysyllabic words anyone has ever heard. You could have an IQ that would make Einstein want to blow you. And in the end, if you are emotionally retarded, I'm better than you. That's all you really need to take away from this. Don't be jealous; but, if you are, don't tell me.

Lesson 3:

Emotional stupidity aside, the human animal is capable of so much stupidity; one wonders if it carries with it some evolutionary advantage. Do stupid people give birth to people with more symmetrical features that are hence more likely to procreate? I don't know. I am not a geneticist. However, there clearly aren't very many deterrents to being stupid. Otherwise, it wouldn't be so omnipresent. The catch 22 in this situation is the fact that stupid people are frequently too stupid to realize they are stupid. What a blissfully ignorant existence!

Hey, that was the second time I used the term "blissfully ignorant existence." Speaking of being blissfully ignorant...

Part 3:
"This Just in, The Mayor of Baltimore Can Melt Snow With Her Thoughts!!!"

Sometimes, stupidity can be temporary. Sometime stupidity isn't localized to the emotions and like the most aggressive of diseases, stupidity can metastasize through a person's being. Sometimes, stupidity is state of being brought on by self-inflicted ignorance. This is a story about that kind of stupidity.

Being from the mid-Atlantic region, I am not terribly used to blizzards. Sure, we get our fair share of snow-fall. But, dump a couple feet of snow in our cities and we start to get a little wonky. Back in the winter of 2010 Baltimore was blanketed with a record amount of snow. As in most unfamiliar situations, most people chose to panic. I chose to dig my car out and go to work. The problem encountered by myself and other logical thinkers was that it took about 4-5 hours to dig our vehicles out. Although there is no assigned parking in the city, the citizens who broke my back digging out spaces wanted them back when they returned home. Many people, myself included, took to marking these spots with a trashcan, lawn chair or any object that clearly states, "This spot is mine. Please don't piggyback off of my shoveling by stealing it."

This is not a terribly new concept and it has pretty much been the accepted practice in many urban environments during a substantial snow fall. Baltimore hasn't recently been known for its leadership and the newest drunk driver to take the wheel of the bus rapidly speeding toward Detroit was a woman who will remain nameless because, I am scared of being sued. To be fair, the city had not seen snow fall like this in a while and the city was ill prepared to get rid of the seemingly insurmountable amount of snow. However, during a radio show that was broadcast well over a week after the snow had ended and well before many of the streets had been plowed even once, the mayor commented that it was "time to bring in the lawn chairs and various markers staking out parking spaces."

Really? What made it "time"? Had there been an unnoticed two day stretch of 40 degree weather that melted all of the mountains of snow that had been blocking all of the parking that wasn't dug out by a private citizen?

The fact is, there was still 10 foot high mounds of snow blocking any parking that has not been dug out by the citizens of any given block. The amount of time since the snow had become rather irrelevant based on the fact that a large amount of the snow had yet to be removed by the city. If parking spaces that were not dug out by citizens began surfacing because of an as then non-existent thaw, then yes it would have been time to bring in our "illegal markers".

The sad truth is, nothing had changed since Baltimore had the big snow except for the fact that one lane had been plowed out of the center of my street. As the mayor continued to spout time passed since the blizzard, I started to wonder if she was just too stupid to realize what was happening. My street had remained both figuratively and literally frozen. Why would my behavior (a behavior deemed perfectly acceptable a week prior) change when nothing else has?

I proudly, and without shame, continued to claim my parking space until something changed on my street. It was quite stupid to expect otherwise. And until I witnessed the mayor take the high heels off and grab a shovel, I was not going to be deterred. I remember listening to this radio broadcast as I drove home passed several of my neighbors hacking away at the Fortress of Solitude that still sat at the end of my block. I personally had and have no problem with this particular mayor; however, I do think that her statement was incredibly stupid. And, on top of that, it was arrogantly stupid. Stating it was time to stop a practice that allowed us to function in the absence of municipal assistance as if the tax-payers had gotten to have their fun and it was time to get serious. What an arrogant and stupid statement to literally broadcast while you were dropping the snow removal ball. During the same time period in which the mayor declared the non-existent "great thaw" had begun, it was pointed out that crime had dropped 70 % and the city went 8 days without a murder. I had no doubt that this was true because all of the criminals were frozen in the iceberg that took out Titanic at the corner of my street.

Again, I don't think this woman to be stupid. I do find her statement, incredibly so. While she was at it, she may as well have written out a decree declaring snow removal "a nice thought" or "something Mother Nature started and will hence take care of herself." We needed actual snow removal, not discussion on how the citizens of Baltimore should react better to the lack of it. Perhaps she could have collected the salt from the tears of everyone who hoped Baltimore was done with ignorant leaders who govern from a nice house in the richer neighborhoods as opposed to walking the streets of a typical neighborhood in order to assist in the thaw. On second thought, the streets weren't very safe to walk with all that snow everywhere.

Lesson 4:

Stupidity is a menace. It is a threat to rational thinking human being everywhere. Unfortunately, it is systemic. Stupidity will survive the human race for several millennia and, sadly, no one is immune, not even me. People who are not necessarily stupid will say and do very stupid things. Shocking as it may be, I myself have, on occasion, acted very stupid. These things are going to happen. Always give the person a chance to recover. Speaking of arrogant stupidity, this provides a rather labored yet usable segue into my next topic...

Part 4:

"Oh, your last name is Smith? I'm afraid you owe us thousands of dollars."

There are so many things that make me want to kick someone in the teeth that occur on a daily basis. I suppose I should not worry about order of importance and simply begin. Now don't get me wrong. Prior to what the previous entries may have lead you to believe, I have nothing against stupid people. It's a disability like any other. It's like being in a wheelchair or having a huge tumor growing out of your ass. The only difference is with stupid people, some of them think they are smart. Now don't get me wrong, it's healthy to have a nice reasonable amount of confidence; however, maybe "these people" should take a moment and make sure their feigned confidence has not become full on arrogance. Some of my best friends are incredibly stupid people and I love them as if they were just like the rest of us; but, the kind of stupid people I have problems with are the ones that speak to me as if I were stupid and they recently graduated from MIT. Allow me to provide an example.

I recently attempted to obtain my college diploma. It has been several years since I graduated and I felt it was time to care. Actually, I didn't care my mother wanted it. But I digress. As I was saying, I went to the appropriate window in the appropriate department located in the appropriate building of my alma-mater and politely asked for my diploma.

Bear in mind it has been several years since I walked across that stage sweating like Whitney Houston on account of it being 5000 degrees in the 40 year old gymnasium the powers that be at my college felt it appropriate in which to hold my graduation. So, I felt it only fair that maybe I should receive a symbol representing that I made it through the festival of hell they call the film program. I asked the nice woman for my diploma and she nicely informed me that I would have to go to the parking fine department first. Instead of asking her a million questions that she would be unable to answer and slapping her snide and acne-scar ridden face, I decided to simply save my rage for the next point on my crusade map.

I arrived at the parking fines office and waited in line for like 6 years. Seriously, had I had a laptop with wireless access with me, I could have gotten my doctorate online in the amount of time it took for them to get to me.

I arrived at the window, grey haired, tired and eligible for social security and I asked, again politely, why my diploma is being kept from me. I realized half-way through the hodge podge of random mono-syllabic words this quarter-whit was spewing out that she was, in fact, an extremely stupid person; however, at this point I was not upset by this. Remember stupidity is a disability.

This particular dumbass informed me that I had an unpaid ticket on my record. I inquired as to specifics and was given the license plate number. I immediately recognized it as my mother's license plate number. At the time, my mother worked for the State Department of Education and was probably there on business one day and got a ticket.

I informed the stupid woman in front of me that the ticket was not mine but was obtained by my mother and further inquired as to how that would even get attributed to me in the first place. Now here is where this person changes simply from being a person suffering from stupidity and becomes now an arrogant stupid person. She leans into the counter and looks at me as if I have just asked her how they find people small enough to fit inside my dashboard and to sing to me in my car while I'm driving, and says,

"Well, the last name....Obviously."

Now it was the "obviously" that made me want to find a way to get through the thick layer of plexi-glass separating me and this moron before me. How dare she act as though I was stupid? "That is ridiculous!" I said.

I further explained that they could not attribute a parking violation to me simply because we share the last name. The inbred lunatic looked at me, starry-eyed, blank-headed and confused.

Suddenly, all the work I had before me flooded my imagination. The hours waiting in line to find out I speaking to the wrong person, the time trying explain to multiple people the situation, the sheer effort that lay before me became too much. I walked away.

Lesson 5:

Like Mick Jagger said, "You can't always get what you want." And you can't always change a bad situation. Someimes, it is just best to walk away, judge the person with whom you had the interaction and live to tell the tale. To this day I have spoken to several other people at the university who are obviously all suffering airborne retardation. To this day, I have never received my diploma. I will keep trying. I have faith that I will encounter someone who can grasp the very simple concept I am trying to relay. Until then, my mother has nothing to hang on her wall. Speaking of my mother, her favorite movie is Steel Magnolias...

Chapter 3
Part 1:
"This One Was Not Bad. It Was Not Bad At All."

The above quote is from Steel Magnolias. Sally Field says it to Julia Roberts' character Shelby after she goes into a diabetic fit, pounds her arm against a chair, freaks out, refuses juice and looks like a big monkey when her lips curl out while she cries (to be fair that is just Julia Roberts' mouth. It isn't Shelby's fault).

My friend says this to me anytime I am interested in someone. This is for good reason; because, anytime I start to realize that I am interested in someone, I have this internal diabetic Shelby that pounds her fist against the cerebral chair in my head and spits orange juice onto poor Truvy's beauty shop floor(just watch the movie).

Before continuing to explain, I should point out that none of this takes place anywhere outside of my head. I keep it internal and do not let the object of my interest *ever* know that this internal shit storm is raging betwixt my rather large yet beautiful ears. While I am aware that I have this fault, I am also aware that it is nobody's burden but my own...and Truvy's...and possible Sally Field's.

I don't want everything to be so difficult. I want to meet someone, have them like me, have me like them and then we can make out and see where things go. Why does it always come down to me biting my nails in anticipation of a rejection that usually comes at my own hand? (I tend to purposely annoy the other person until they go away). Then I actually feel relieved. The internal Shelby has finally swallowed enough juice to make her "start making some sense" and the fit subsides. Now, loyal reader, you may be thinking to yourself, "He shouldn't blame himself this much. He is being so introspective and looking to himself to fix this problem. This isn't cynicism." (Actually you are probably saying, "I can't believe I am stuck in this full body cast and this is the only book my caretaker had on hand." But I digress).

Have no fear. I am still me. (Sidebar: what the fuck does that mean when singers name their albums that or some derivative thereof? "You're still you." "I'm still me." No shit...Really?. I am going to cut an album entitled, "Holy shit, I'm Cher!").

Anyway, I am still going to blame everyone on the outside...mostly, because it tickles me to do so. I am almost entirely attracted to emotional retards. They just broke up with someone and are unaware that they are just filling a lonely void until they date me for a week and run into their ex at a party and they realize they aren't over them. No shit. I could have told you that, if you hadn't lied to me about when you all broke up. Or, they only like the part of the interaction that is flirtatious and fun and then once they might feel anything...anything at all, they get all weird and I get impatient and just want to go home and force-feed "Shelby" some juice. (Play Xbox.)

My point, and I barely have one at this point, is that I am a cynic. I'm a punk and I criticize people to the point of demoralization the way other people shake hands. But, I want to find someone who enjoys that sort thing. Wow, that person is going to be so fucked up! I can't wait!

Until then, I sit, hair a mess, the orange juice on my clothes becoming a sticky reminder of monkey lips forming on my face and Sally Field softly whispering, "This one was not bad. It was not bad at all." Thanks Sally. Sorry about Smokey and the Bandit 2.

Lesson 6:
Like it or not we are all just trying to survive here. Trying to find love can be a truly harrowing experience. Our feelings get hurt and our guns get shy. Every single heart that has been broken is damaged. Don't take shit from anyone. But, if you find a person who is worth it, don't miss out on something potentially awesome because their past keeps making

them do stupid things. Despite our impressive location on the evolutionary ladder, we are still animals. Our past traumas frequently dictate our future instincts. Assume the other person has been through just as much as you have. Give them a chance to change. But, don't wait too long. There is a line from the movie Kissing a Fool that applies pretty well,"Love cannot be found where it doesn't exist, nor can it be hidden where it truly does." Speaking of movies no one has seen but me...

Part 2:
"These Are My Choices? You? or Lana? Or Joan?"

While I am on the subject of movies that dudes shouldn't like that I happen to love, (the transitions are getting shameful at this point) one of my favorite movies of all time is Postcards from the Edge. Without getting *way* gay and going into in depth explanation of the plot, there is a scene in the movie where Shirley MacLaine is talking to Meryl Streep, who plays her daughter, and says,

"How would you like to have Joan Crawford for a mother..or Lana Turner?"

Meryl Streep replies,

"These are my choices? You? Or Lana? Or Joan?"

This quote comes up a lot in my life; because, I keep finding myself saying things like, "At least I don't have cancer." I mean it. I am grateful for the lack of deadly disease and the general health of me and mine. But, I must say, it was getting a little old being grateful for not having a disease. My life had become something of which I have to constantly look on the bright side. I find myself missing being a child. Not that I long for the days of constant nasal congestion and prepubescent confusion. But, I do miss generally believing that people were good at heart and the world was a good place. Part of me feels like a shit. If Ann Frank could do it, why can't I? Because, I am spoiled that is why. But, I am what I am. So, the section about people pissing on my parade continues.

Contrary to the perception of most people, I am an incredibly optimistic person. This optimism means that I am constantly having my hopes crapped on; until I decided not to have expectation (See chapter 1). It seem as though people today cannot live up to the lowest of expectations. I am not a needy guy. I don't need to be coddled or treated like glass. But, I have this inflated sense of justice. I believe that the world is completely unfair and we should, when we can, strive to make things as fair as possible.

I don't think it is fair that the woman with no teeth who lives 4 houses down from me can scream outside her house for 30 minutes to be let in at 4 am and nothing happens; while, if I slam my car door too hard my fart-knocking neighbor calls the police. I find it completely unjust that a woman at work comes in 4 hours a week and lies about making up time on the weekends and I get spoken too about coming in on the weekends to make up a sick day. I find it really dumb that ignorant people who float through life on the intelligence of others live a much more blissful existence than those of us who have the brain power to look at the world from other people's perspectives could ever hope to experience.

All these aspects of the adult human experience bother me on a daily basis. That having been said, I find a balance somewhere. I see that while aspects of my life suck, many aspects don't. I am aware that while I am bitching about my job, someone is complaining (and rightfully so) about not having one at all and not being able to feed their family.

The life of a cynic is one of relativity. You have to remember other people are suffering worse than you are while still being really pissed off about your own suffering. Own your anger about how life poops in your punch bowl. But, never forget those that are constipated and cannot poop at all.

Lesson 7:

Sometimes we are met with awful choices. It can happen a lot. But, those moments, they remind you that you are alive. When you are 80 you will be able to say, "I lived, dammit." And you will know you lived because you made the hard choices and you're still here. In short, I say, "These are my choices [for a mother]? You? Or Lana? Or Joan?" and then I think. "Yeah, but any of the three are better than not being born at all." Speaking of being born, being a New Year's baby must suck. And on that note, we talk about leaving the old year behind...

Part 3:
"Hey 2010, Suck it!"

New Years Eve can be a particular difficult holiday for a true cynic. Yes, it is full of happy hopes and resolutions and rainbows and kittens. But, the fact is, most of the time, the same shit happens all over again. You have already learned not to have expectations and that most people are stupid. It is with these skills that you will learn to make New Years Eve bearable. In the following passage I will be dealing with the year 2010 because, a) it was last year and b) it fits well with this chapter and I am not terribly creative. Regardless, these are universal truths that can be applied timelessly.

Every new year I like to start by telling the year before to suck it. When yet another year has gone the way of the bellbottoms, jelly bracelets and Farah Fawcette hair, it is usually time to reflect. But you might be saying to yourself,

"Wait, those are 3 examples of cyclical things."

Well loyal reader, you are correct. Unlike Angelina Jolie and her lip balm, I chose these 3 things wisely. (Her lips always look like she has spent a couple weeks walking through the desert without water; but, I digress).

I am not sure about you; but my 2010 was a year of the circle. Things that in 2009 to which I had bid farewell, seemed to come back around. I do not choose the word "resurfaced" for a couple reasons. Firstly, that word implies that I buried or "sank" something that is now coming back to haunt me. Anyone who knows me knows I bury nothing. I may detonate, tear asunder, even devour if the situation warrants; but never, never do I choose to not deal with and to bury something. Secondly, when something resurfaces, it is the same thing that went down. Unchanged, (save a few barnacles or some moss) the same object re-emerges.

The things that came back around for me in 2010 had evolved, metamorphosed, if you will(And you will because you do). Sometimes, from a caterpillar, emerged a butterfly. And sometimes, from a nuclear mishap, emerged a horrible mutant bent on mindless destruction and dissemination of its nuclear induced zombification virus.

I had let go of some things in 2009. I had, at great cost to my own heart (and at moments, my own sanity), cut loose ties with more than one really wonderful yet damaging person. People aren't black and white. I mean, they are but not for the purposes of this exercise. Anyway, people aren't usually one thing or the other. They aren't good or bad or selfish or kind. They oscillate around in this fluid state "acting" in certain ways. They act selfish. They act kindly. Sometimes, they act with complete lack of regard for other beings. Some people do that last one a lot. Sometimes, after a while, these "actions" begins to define them. No matter what you knew of them or who you knew them to be, their actions have begun to cause their fluid state to solidify.

Will it always be solid? You don't know. But you know that there is now a rock where you need a river and you have to let go...again, this time of the possibilities of a future source of water. This rock is here *now* and that future river is no longer visible to the mind's eye. The rock-person (80's Saturday morning cartoon imagery aside) was already long gone. The hope that I hadn't realized remained had to now follow.

There were good transformations in 2010 as well. People of whom I had let go returned with new understanding, new peace and new offerings of friendship. Truly reconnecting is a divine thing and it is something for which I have always been grateful. There is no better feeling than simply letting go and starting fresh. Ripping down the dry wall and tearing out the kitchen but sticking with the same foundation, if you will. (And you will because you do.)

I changed in 2010. I began to feel this hope. Not that I had been devoid of it before; but this time, the hope was permanent. I began to realize that all the crap I had dealt with, every boss I had ever had being just awful, my love life being the stuff sitcoms are made of, my luck being not so much Irish as Somalian, had all unwittingly prepared me for anything. I can handle pretty much any situation, no matter how crazy, because I have seen this shit before.

Hey crazy bum on the street running towards me when there are literally 12 other people you could have chosen, no problem! I know what to do now! Hey spoiled tenant who purposely leaves the lights and heat on just to "get your money's worth" when you barely pay anything for what you have, great job! Here are the want ads, find yourself your dream home and don't let the door hit you where the good lord evicted you because you were too ungrateful.

Hey bone chip in my wrist snapping off because I walked outside and my tire was flat and I tried to change it quickly in the hopes of not being late to work resulting in my missing a whole day anyway to get x-rayed, so what? I am a multi-tasker. I can email my boss that I'm in urgent care while I am being shown the triangular bone chip that had been hiding in my wrist like dormant herpes sore for 20 years. Bring it!

Hey wonderful new job that came just in time to save me from poverty, so what that my new boss sexually harasses me and has literally forced me to punch him in the stomach! So fucking what! I have a mean right hook. (Now that my wrist has healed...kind of.)

In actuality, 2010 was one of the most dichotomous years of my entire life. While it was easily the hardest year for me to date, it was also the year that gave birth to the pillar of emotional stability and shining example of psychic philanthropy that you see before you (yes, I am aware you can't see me).

In a lot of ways, this year sucked a fat one. On the other hand, so many awesome things have come out of the giant mount of shit I was forced to sift through for the last 12 months. I am in school. I have a job I can tolerate that pays me just enough. I am on better terms with everyone in my life and I think my dog and I have finally come to a mutual understanding . I have a lot to cover here.

First, I would like to point out that Baltimore smells a little less like rotten shrimp than in the days past and I am appreciative of this fact. As an outspoken fan of this wonderful city, I also am very aware of its faults. I am aware that my feet barely touch the actually sidewalk outside Sip & Bite on Boston Street because I am gliding on a colorful cushion of cigarette butts. I am aware that if I don't hear a siren blaring past my window every couple of minutes, I will know I have gone deaf. (Incidentally, this also causes my dog to go all "Call of the Wild" and howl like an asshole for 15 minutes) .

I am undeniably aware that the guy peeing on the side of the Royal Farms might one day decide he has had enough and attempt to rape my car. All this aside, I love the city when it snows. I love that I can walk to a bar with a small amount of effort and run into at least one of my sister's alcoholic friends drowning their "sorrows" in a glass....or 12. I love that every day this city gets better and, in some way, makes huge strides in improving itself. I do very much love the city of Baltimore. I love it, even though I sleep with a stun gun and carry an extendable baton. While I love it, I limit my ignorant expectations to my love life.

I would like to examine the job I obtained in 2010. Oh sure, I can't talk specifically about because I worked in National Security. I can; however, say that I laugh at something every day. I am both grateful and disturbed by this fact simultaneously. I work across the hall from my father, who is nice enough to call me every morning to tell me I am "almost late" when I do not arrive at work by 7:30. This, I have explained several times to my loving father that "almost late" translates to the sane as "on time." Furthermore, I am not late until 9:30. This amusing little aspect of my occupation is magnified by the fact that my father wakes up at 3 in the morning to get to work and get a good parking space. Plus he is done work by 12. I wish I had that determination. Grey Goose vodka sees to it I rarely get up before 6am.

As I mentioned previously, several of my interpersonal relationships came to official end during the year of 2010. Without going into further detail, selfish people faded away. It was really hard to say goodbye and truly end these chapters to my life. That having been said, I no longer get stressed when I try to figure out what I am doing on any given night. I don't feel guilty for wanting to stay in or feel pressured to spend time with one person and not another. I no longer feel like a child being pulled in several different directions by the insecurities of the people with whom I chose to spend aspects of my life. The people remaining have found a balance with me. I also drink a lot more than I used to and I find no shame in this.

My house has truly become my home. I reside in the majority of the house and my renter resides in the smaller portion. This is a drastic change from my former life. I enjoy coming home and aside from my asshole quadruped roommate that periodically decides to crap on my dining room floor or chew on my couch, my roommates are cool.

The holidays just wrapped up and I have to say that no one cried or left angry from any of the family functions. So kudos, Dunkle family. I, once again, displayed by gaming prowess and lack of a functional social life when I single handedly held my own against my entire family while playing the board game, "Scene It." I rejoiced in my victory and then cringed when I realized how many TV shows and Movies I truly watch. I am not sure any human being is meant to be exposed to that much media. Thank God I don't read or I might truly have a problem.

All the niceness aside, it wouldn't be the Christmas season if I didn't wish some yuletide hell on those that have wronged me. 2010 was such a trying year that I decided to make a Holiday Hit List. Enjoy!

To my former tenant who still owes me over $1300, I hope your tree catches fire and in your drunken/high state you throw a glass of pure vodka on it only exacerbating the situation. Aside from being a metaphor for your entire life, this action would also result in the loss of your eye brows and nose hair. I wish these two things for the following reasons. I hope you lose your eyebrows because I hope everyone laughs when they see you walking around looking like Whoopi Goldberg. I wish the nose hair loss on you because it will, if my dreams ever come true, result in a chronic sinus infection that you can never have treated. Eat shit you useless waste of skin. Merry Christmas!

To my nerdy bastard of a neighbor who stressed me out this year by calling the city hotline because I didn't bring my trashcans in soon enough or because I waited 5 minutes before shoveling my sidewalk during a blizzard. I hope you lose all control of your blatter in the following year. I hope that you are forced to refrain from ingesting liquids after 3pm in order to avoid rendering your mattress a urine soaked representation of the misery you have caused those that live near you. I hope that Santa poops in your mouth. Merry Christmas!

To my rebound relationship that I stupidly fooled myself into believing was worth my time in the beginning of this year, I hope your life continues exactly as it has since your birth. Oddly enough, this is my meanest yuletide curse yet!

To all those people who used my moments of weakness to make themselves feel better for a second. I hope that others return the kindness you have shown me. I hope that when you are sitting at home bathing in the warm glow of the lights hanging from your tree that you catch a glimpse in the mirror. Merry Christmas!!

So, to wrap it all up, I say goodbye to the past year. If this year had been a person, I would kick it swiftly in the balls and light its hair on fire. Then I would thank it. I am stronger. I think.

I have truly been able to relax in a fashion I have not yet known. I realized, no matter what, no matter whom, no matter the lack of validation I receive, I am going to be fine. I will struggle. I will borrow money (a crap load from my mother and sister). I will sell DVD's for champagne and vodka when the need arises. I have emerged from 2010 in Star Wars style...with a new hope!

Don't get me wrong. The title of this section remains prudent. 2010, like most of my recent years, was rough. It smacked me around a little bit. And, while I respect it for keeping its hoes in line, New Years' pimp hand gets a little heavy every once in a while. So 2010, I say to you, "Suck it! I'll see you next year."

Lesson 8:

When things come to an end, it is natural to examine them. You will find yourself doing this at the end of movies, trips, relationship, etc. But, when the year comes to an end everyone looks forward and makes resolutions. This is a good practice. But, make sure to take a minute and look back. Think about what you survived that year. Think about what you got to experience. Make a vow that the following year will have more or less of whatever you loved or hated about the previous year. It can't all happen at once; but, it is within your control to draw things towards you. While we are on the subject of parties, (well New Years) I have encountered a lot of cynicism inducing behavior at social gatherings. So, I thought I might abuse yet another segue and move on to...

Part 4:
"Sir, While I Appreciate Your Fervor, You Have Smacked Me Three Times and Spit On My Cheek Twice During Your Completely Unnecessary Gesticulation!"

I am noticing an increasing number of hyperactive adults. This is starting to really ware on my ever-fraying patience. You know what I'm talking about. That guy at the party who *thinks* he is the life of it. When in actuality, everyone is just fascinated with how inappropriate someone of that age and weight could possibly be.

I am talking about the man who listens intently to what you are saying, not to the point of what you are saying, just each individual sentence, so that he can pick one statement out and make a "funny" comment.

I am talking about the man who proceeds to get drunk by 8pm and acts the way everyone else at the party is reserving for 2am. I am talking about the man, who if you happen to have an outdoor affair on some kind of heightened platform such as a deck or a rooftop, proceeds to find someone walking on the street that will find it the least funny and yell things at them.

I am talking about the guy who cannot help himself from saying the most inappropriate thing possible and then not picking up the non-verbal cue of everyone staring at the ground until someone starts another conversation. (Or worse, instead of just letting pass and letting another conversation start, he says, "Oh I'm sorry. Was that offensive? I didn't mean to offend you...blah blah blah.)

I am speaking of the gentleman who screams constantly in a bar despite the fact that the people he is talking to are maybe a foot away from him.

I am talking about the guy who tells the worst stories; but, tells them with an intensity that should be reserved for dictators or pirates. (Two different kinds of intensity. Take your pick.) They relay the worst story ever with a tenacity that causes their arms to flail about and little droplets of spit to carpet bomb your arm, the top of your hand or worse, your face.

These are children's behavior characteristics, people. These are things CHILDREN do that illicit phrases like,

"Indoor voice." ("Shut Up!" if you were one of my older siblings.)...or...

"We don't say things like that to people, sweetie." ("Get out of here, Randy!")...or...

"You don't need to say EVERYTHING you think, son." (or "Ya see? THIS is why we always tell you to shut up or get out of here,Randy!")

These behaviors (and the many other that I don't have time to list) make life harder on everyone. When someone's little brother acts like this, it is understandable, he/she is a child. When adults act like this, it is unacceptable; he/she is a douche bag.

These people know no shame. They interact just enough to be obnoxious; but, remain coherent enough if you try to entertain yourself by mocking them. It is a sad part of any cynics like. But, when this guy or gal enters the party, grab your drink of choice, make for higher ground and try to survive.

Lesson 9:

We have all encountered "that guy". It is just a matter of recognizing the signs and avoiding him/her. However, these people are the road not taken. As annoying as they are, they are simply a product of crippling insecurity turned inside out. It would be easy to give in to your urges and humiliate them. But, they are already doing that to themselves and, in the end, it is actually kind of sad. But at least these people don't refrain from taking an opinion on something while reaping the same benefits as those who have chosen a side. See what I did there?...

Chapter 4
Part 1:
"The fence you're riding is rotting out from under you."

You have learned to navigate stupidity, to lower your expectations and to deal with life's little pit falls. But, as a professional cynic, I have encountered a problem present in so many people that I must address with you. For the following passage, I will use Gay rights. But, the spirit of what I am saying should be obvious. We live in a society of flip-floppers, a whirlpool of sliding positions and malleable conviction. Aside from being an empty existence, this is no way for a cynic to live.

I personally have had it. In this endless sea of politicians trying to either blatantly deny other American's their rights or ride that shaky fence and not state an opinion one way or another it is time to take a side.

I tend to avoid the topic of Gay rights only because I have such a hand in it, that I cannot appear un-biased. However, I have found myself growing steadily sicker of people either avoiding the topic because it doesn't affect them or unabashedly being in favor of keeping others from being happy.

This may seem trite but for God's sake, gay people want to marry. How is this a major issue to anyone other than the parties that want to marry? I would understand if gay people wanted to marry a straight person, or a car, or if they wanted to make everyone gay. That would be outrageous. Anyone campaigning for that should be beaten severely.

But when people just want to commit to one another and that is opposition of the government (a government that should be totally and only concerned with the ridiculous way in which it has been managed of late) we have an issue...a rather large, colorful and tastefully decorated issue.

I understand it from politicians; because, they ride the fence or take a Gestapo-esque position against anything that may jeopardize their upcoming elections. I understand it. I think it is reprehensible because people are still being denied the right to live freely in a country that supposedly prides itself on being the "land of the free" ;but, I understand it. The politicians will never do anything just because it is the right thing to do. I know this. But I will say this anyway. Gay marriage is nothing but good for economy.

Politicians should avoid topics like morality, because if any of them open their proverbial desk drawers one would find naked pictures of children, receipts proving misappropriation of funds, a mistress' phone number or just a big bag of porn. In some, if not most cases in which these idiots are campaigning to stand in the way of gay unions, you will find a gay lover's phone number.

There are only two reasons to be against gay rights. A) Religion and B) You are gay yourself or worried your son or daughter is and you are letting that cloud your political maneuvers. The problem with these reasons are as follows:

A) It is nothing short of wrong and immoral to make governmental decisions based on religious principles when it is the right of every citizen of that country not to believe in anything (...and a cynics mantra).

B) The fact that you or your son or daughter might be a big dyke or a flamer is not the gay communities' problem. Deal with it you big fairy! It's not about you. It's about the American people you laughingly pretend to represent and care about.

There we have covered politicians. Good, that's done. Now let's cover regular average Joe and Jane Q. Public. These people make me sick! Take a fucking side! You don't get to ride the fence and stay there until you know who the winning side is and then say, "I am a supporter." The fence was the supporter, you were the muther fucker putting weight on it. I have made a decision. That decision is that no one in my life will be ambiguous any longer. Ambiguity can be a cynic's worst enemy and it must be avoided at all costs.

If you are for gay rights, say it! If you are against it, good then say it. You cannot be "friends" with someone and secretly (or openly) believe they are wrong for being who they are. Just like you couldn't be friends with a black person and then help your husband put that pretty white sheet over his head in the 60's. What a bunch of fucking cowards! At least the people with the white hoods have taken them off and call themselves "Evangelical Christians" now.

It makes me sick (not to mention sad) that anyone professing love for God would want to deny other people happiness. Finding joy in cynicism can be a challenge and anyone chipping away at other sources of smiley faces and rainbows is messing with a delicate balance. This is a shot in the dark; but, I'm quite certain God wants people to be happy. Or maybe he just wants people to hate each other and handle snakes and quote a really unclear and metaphorical book to prove they know what he wants, and blame natural disasters on the people living in the place where they occur and bomb clinics where most of the people inside have a huge chance of being teenagers and judge everyone but themselves and get caught in hotel rooms with women with really bad hair and religiously persecute other people and call it "Patriotism" or "Spreading Democracy". I don't know. I'm not a Theologian.

My favorite response to the issue of Gay Rights is "I don't care one way or another. It doesn't affect me." Well glad to know you aren't completely narcissistic or anything. Are you kidding me with this? It does affect you. Because the minute these idiots find a passage in the bible that relates to morons with their heads up their asses, you will be next. Our last president thought he was a prophet! What is going on?!! People, please imagine with me, the minute *W* admitted to hearing instructions from God during an interview, the camera cut to heaven and God looked up from his bologna sandwich with a look of surprise and said, "Wait, What?"

Not to mention, even if it doesn't affect you, what's going on is wrong and that should affect you. It should eat away at your sense of patriotism and your sense of responsibility as a human being. These are your brethren, whether you are exactly like them or not. The statement that it doesn't affect every single American makes me want to piss on people. (Which I should have every right to do...if he's into that.)

Lesson 10:

Sometimes, being a cynic is being angry. If you call yourself someone's friend then make sure you support the way they live. If you don't then you aren't a friend. You are a hypocrite. If you don't hide your ignorance, then get out your white sheets, fire hoses and German shepherds because a fight is coming and God is sick of you using his name for what you are doing. Friends in this world are hard to come by. It is a travesty to pretend to be one when you aren't. If you are someone doing this right now, stop it. If you are someone who has a "friend" doing this, stop letting it happen. And for those of you on that fence, you might want get off. The other cynics and I are about to drive our cars through it.

On the subject of driving...(that one was not half bad.)

Part 2:

"Come on, Sally. Let's go take a joyride and kill some people."

If you are afraid, apprehensive, slow witted, have bad reflexes or are just too old to exist I submit to you that maybe you should re-evaluate whether you should operate heavy machinery. I know it is a radical idea. But, hear me out. If you have some kind of condition or you are very old, what makes you think that you can drive a huge steal weapon down the street? Either you are dangerous because you are an idiot behind the wheel of a machine that has the potential to kills dozens in a matter of minutes, or you are in danger of me making you victim # 1 because you're driving in the left lane at 30 miles an hour and avoiding eye contact with me as I pass you and wonder why you are still alive. Bad drivers please hear me.

Cars, in general, are dangerous things. Think about it. You are steering a huge metal box around on four wheels at 60-80 miles per hour with nothing to stop you but four pads pressed against 4 tires rotating at incredibly high velocities powered by nothing but your right foot. We haven't come far from the Flintstone method of stopping a car and I for one do not want to die.

Although they are not the only culprits, I use the elderly as an example of people who should not drive because...well...it's the easiest and I'm lazy.

I remember very clearly being in the backseat of my grandparent's huge tank of a car while they took me to the store or the movies or some other destination over 5 miles away and hence far enough to have the potential of risking my life. My grandparents were not young people. My parents were not young when they had me and my grandparents were not young when they had them and hence, I was young but my grandparents were past driving age. I remember multiple instances where I sat, too young to drive yet old enough to recognize the fault of a near miss lay in the driver of the very car in which I was housed, while my grandparents complained about the young drivers and how they are "menaces" on the road.

As we get older, our reflexes dull, our hearing fades and our vision blurs; and yet, our licenses just keep getting renewed. Am I really the only person who has thought of this?

Lesson 11:

Perhaps once we as human beings reach a point where we cannot do what we once did quite as well, we should do less of it. When we start doing badly at work, maybe it is time for a career change. When we start taking things out on our kids, maybe it is time for a break and some adult time. And, at a certain age, when we start operating vehicles less efficiently, we should have to renew our licenses every year. I submit to you the possibility that offending old people might not be as important as the prevention of old people killing other people. I know this sounds just crazy. But, my reflexes aren't what they used to be and I am worried that one of these days, I am going to be unable to swerve out of the way of a 1986 Buick Skylark as it is steered in my lane by an elderly person who just remembered where they were going and has to hurry up and get over to the right lane because their exit is coming up in 10 miles.

Speaking of killing people...

Part 3:
"Open letters from my closed mind."

The human race is conspiring to slowly kill me via exposing me to the most annoying people ever to walk the face of the earth and raising my blood pressure and hence leading me to an early grave.

There are hundreds of things that drive me crazy and help me rocket down the slippery slope to cynicism. However, there are a select few that really require me to do the emotional equivalent of the "pee pee dance" to keep from hurting people in public. I have prepared a list of people to whom I would like to write open letters...

1) An open letter to anyone scanning coupons at the SuperFresh at 4am in the morning who cannot figure out how to use the self-check out lane and shouldn't have your children out this late.

Dear Asshole,

The whole reason I come here at this hour is to avoid those of you who herd yourself into grocery stores in abundance during waking hours. You mothers in their tight t-shirts and love handles holding a baby in one arm and buying a carton of lucky strikes with the other are stuff my nightmares are made of and I come in here late to avoid you specifically. But, in I walk at an ungodly hour and there you are coughing into open air and screaming at your children in the self check-out line(which incidentally you stare at as though you had just been rocketed thousands of years into the future and asked to helm a star-ship).

If you have 8 billion coupons, more power to you. You should be saving your money. Spend it on hair removal or the medication for the VD your child will inevitably contract once they are a teenager. But, for God's sake, have your coupons ready and know how to work the machine.

I'm tired of watching you Devry flunk-outs repeatedly tap the same button and become so impatient that you go faster than the computer can think and hence are constantly responding to things in an incorrect order. For instance, the screen says, "Please push the button corresponding to your payment method". But, you, Queen Fry-hair push the "cash" button and then grow impatient and push it eight more times hence responding to the next 8 questions that followed the "payment method" inquiry and end up just needing to start over. Meanwhile, I am sitting with one carton of toothpaste ready to beat you with your own child. Why?

Sincerely,

A concerned citizen.

2) An open letter to those idiots making no effort to corral your children while adults who didn't bring forth one of the most annoying beings known to man are trying to eat, talk or just exist in public.

Dear Procreator,

I refer to your not as a parent because, parents would never stand for the kind of behavior I have to watch you cultivate on an almost daily basis. Really, children misbehave. I am aware of this. My problem is your child is clearly screaming in public, clearly disturbing the adults around you, undeniably making it impossible for those of us unlucky enough to be stuck on a bus, in a restaurant or standing in line with you, to think of anything except walking over, slapping your child across the face and then slapping you with the other hand for not disciplining your child. Teach the child now that the world will not put up with his/her bullshit. Trust me, I know people who are learning that lesson in their 20's and 30's. Everyone hates them.

Sincerely,

A better parent than you, although I have no children.

3) An open letter to people who work in the service industry but clearly shouldn't.

Dear Jerk,

If you cannot count, grasp basic concepts or don't like working with people yet insist on working at a bank, car dealership or any job relating to money, people, animals, goods, food services or retail, then you probably should reconsider your career endeavors. If you count slower than a fat kid divvying up his Halloween candy, perchance bank teller wasn't the right fit for you.

If you don't like working at Banana Republic, quit. Don't give me attitude because I ask you to let me into a fitting room hence forcing you to postpone your argument with the other flamer behind the counter regarding whether turtle necks are in or out.

If you hate children, perhaps you shouldn't be working as a high school librarian. [You know who you are and I haven't forgotten that you were mean to me!]

If you are just stupid or nasty in general, think of a career that does not involve dealing with other people, medical testing subject comes to mind.

Sincerely,

I hate people. Which is why I work in IT.

4) An open letter to those of you who cannot avoid speaking to people like they are stupid or treating them badly simply because English is not their first language.

Dear Jimbo,

This one bugs me the most. I am impatient as hell. Even I realize that these people are hard-working. What makes me realize this, you ask. The fact that they are able to speak English at all. It is an incredibly difficult language to learn and they make a living and have to deal with assholes like you in a country totally welcoming on paper and totally alienating in actual practice.

In actuality, "these people" are most likely smarter than you will ever hope to be, so drop the attitude, don't speak louder, simply speak clearly and slowly and smile, dammit! The person you are speaking to has dealt with three assholes like you before lunch and probably has a PhD in Neurobiology. I am sure it didn't ruin your day too much that you had to choose English at the ATM.

Sincerely,

Señor Reasonable.

Lesson 12:

It is a natural human reaction to look at everything from only our point of view. It is completely natural to look at the world through "me" colored glasses and get irritated. I might have done it once or twice in the previous section. But, it is our duty to not always go with this instinct. Everyone on this planet struggles at some point. They may be at this point when you encounter them.

Speaking of points, I have one to make about automated things...

Part 4:

"Jimmy's house of automated bullshit, how can I help you?"

I hate almost anything automated. I hate it when I call information and say something and hear "Martha the soulless telephone assistant" repeat something similar to what I said and then say, "Is that right?" And then when I tell the bitch it's not right, she repeats something even less similar to what I said and asks again, condescendingly this time, "Is that right?"

No, bitch, it's not right. Forward me to someone who has genitals!

It's not that I hate automated phone answerers in general. They are useful. When minimum wage earning, quarter-wits that answer the phone in most these places are busy filing their 8 inch nails or hitting on the girl with her thong showing in the next cubicle, it helps to have someone there to make sure the call gets answered. But, it would be nice if they hadn't gotten rid of the option to bypass this "service". There is no longer the option of dialing "0" for the operator. There is no longer the option of holding for a live attendant. That particular freedom has been usurped.

We live in a world with ever crumbling customer service. It isn't as if the person I would be routed to (should I be given that option) would be polite. But at least, when I told him or her to suck a bag of dicks, I could have the satisfaction of hearing them take offense. As it stands, I am required to listen to this poorly manufactured piece of technology. How can this be possible? How can the option to speak to live people no longer exist? I'm sure there are people with a specialized form of agoraphobia who hate to speak to people and who breath a huge sigh of relief whenever Martha picks up the phone; but, are we really catering to these people? Do we really have to let Martha speak to us all as if we were the stupid ones because she can't understand the words, "AMC Theatres" and asks if you want the number to "Peter's House of Pancakes"

Just because Johnny Mouth breather feels uncomfortable with "performing" for live people on the other end of the phone, you *will* speak to Martha! She will eventually get what you said right. You *will* repeat it 95 times in 4 minutes and eventually actually call her a bitch to which she will respond, "Conner and Switch Law Firm...Is that right?" No, Martha, that isn't right. It isn't right at all.

Lesson 13:

Be as cynical as you want; but, never forget that the more as a society that we keep others at arm's length the more we slide toward horrible ends. People are not perfect. Therefore, the things they design are not perfect. Hence, the automated systems people design to help with problems with the other things people have designed are never going to account for every problem the other people who are using said system might encounter. There has to be a way to fix what has gone wrong. The people responsible must start to feel some sort of responsibility. If not, Martha wins. Speaking of taking personal responsibility...

Chapter 5
Part 1:
"It' Called A Condom. Look It Up!"

No, this entry is not going to be solely about birth control. I just felt the title spoke to a disturbing mindset I am beginning to observe in my generation. Thousands upon thousands of the useless around my age are finding themselves with incredibly easily avoidable problems. Pregnancy and genital warts barely scratch the cervix. Credit problems, bankruptcy, miserable marriages, ugly or spoiled children, ugly and spoiled children, all could have been easily avoided if some of these stupid assholes (the future of our country) would just think five minutes in the future. "What does he mean by that?", some of you may find yourself asking. If you are one of these people, then you're an idiot.

But since I have nothing better to do and the previous paragraph, left by itself, makes for a shitty chapter in a book, I will elaborate.. If you make $2,800 a month and your rent is $800, your utilities are $200, your food costs you $200 a month and you have a car payment and insurance payment of $350 a month, you are left a nice chunk of change equaling $1250. Oh wait, we forgot to factor in student loans. So, there goes another $150 or so. Eventually, we are left with $1100 per month to do with as you please. You could put it away in a high yield savings account or a retirement plan. You could make double payments on your student loans in order to be debt free sooner. You could even go out and buy that $900 TV you have been eyeing. Hell, if you want, you could just divide it into a weekly sum of $250 and get blasted with your friends 4 nights a week.

But, will you? Will you do any of these things? Not if you are one of the morons I am speaking about. The moron makes $2800 per month and lives in an $1100 apartment, pays $300 utility bills because his/her mother made him/her turn off the lights when they were little and they are not going to be controlled anymore, and pays $350 a month in food because they are lazy and never learned to cook so they eat out nightly. They pay a car payment of $450 because they bought an Escalade when they graduated instead of a crappy 91 Honda Accord, in which they have to bang the side panel to get the speakers to work because nothing I buy ever works right. But I digress.

You may be saying, "But, Randy, this leaves these fine young ladies and gentlemen with $600 per month. That isn't a lot; but, these people have the right to spend their money any way they like without being judged by bored, bitter people like yourself. The choices they make are their business and who are you to judge them?" Well, if you are one of the people saying this, let me say that you are really long winded and you could have stated that more succinctly.

Furthermore, you are right. If I were to stop here, then yes, this could be viewed as unfair; however, we have not yet fully explored the subject. I have more characteristics that will help illuminate my stupid little peers.

The stupid members of my "generation" will take this remaining $600 and spend it on stupidity. The stupid people will still buy that $900 TV on what intelligent people call "credit" and what these stupid people call "I don't have to worry about it right now." They will also get drunk and have sex with random people. (A practice in and of itself I have no problem with. I just don't understand the propensity for it to be unprotected.) These dumb people will contract genital warts, herpes, chlamydia, gonorrhea, or AIDS and spend the remainder of their monthly $600 on medications to treat the above, or they do the worst thing possible and procreate. Nothing endangers this world of incredibly stupid individuals more than the prospect of even more incredibly stupid individuals dominating it. It isn't so much all people who get into debt problems. Some people just didn't get it and learned from their mistakes and are working hard to overcome it. These clearly are not the individuals of which I speak.

It's not just money, people. Every damn day I get cut off by a stupid, dumb, waste of skin driving a car with the clear belief that no one else in the entire world bothered to buy a car and get their license. I find myself honking my horn and screaming to someone that they are a "Dumb Bitch!" or to "Use your fucking blinker, asshole!". Every time, they look at me with the same look of badly misplaced confidence and wonderment. The big problem? Nine times out of ten, there is at least one child in the back seat.

Let's say that being an idiot and commanding a 2000 lb vehicle on a major road is not enough to piss you off. How about being an incredibly large monkey and running a company, or a theatre, or a country! That's right. That's my main problem. These assholes seem to be lucky. This is a dangerous situation people! This has to be controlled. I can't do everything. I have to work 3 jobs because I have a huge car payment, I can't afford my mortgage, I am about to buy a flat screen TV and on top of all this, the price of Valtrex just went up.

Lesson 14:

Those of us around my age who were raised correctly are going to have a rough time of it. We are going to be running the world alongside those that were raised to believe they are entitled. They are going to live how they live and there will be no bringing them around. It is for this reason that the responsibility falls on the rest of us to live spectacular lives filled with enlightenment and knowledge. We will earn what we receive and for that, what we receive will be so much better. Speaking of badly raised children...

Part 2:

"On the fifth day of Christmas my true love gave to me...five narcissistic kids!"

Christmas just passed while I was writing this book and with the tinsel and pine needles filling up my vacuum, my thoughts drifted to all those children opening presents and sucking the oxygen out of the room.

I have ranted before about parents who don't curb their children when it is clearly appropriate to do so. I was having a conversation with a co-worker yesterday about how she was worried about her child being an only child because she didn't want her to think that the world revolved around her. I loved this. I was, for once, truly relieved that someone was concerned that their perfect little angel has a lot of potential to grow up to be one perfect pain in the fucking asshole. I told her that because she was keeping it in mind, her child probably wouldn't end up that way.

When I was a child and I would come home and tell my mother that I had had a fight with whatever little crumb snatcher I was running around with at the time, my mother would always inquire, "Well, what did *you* do?"

She never allowed me to assume that I was right simply because I was the only one there to defend myself. I learned that lesson because she questioned me. I am noticing a sickening trend among people my age to think that when a conflict arises, they are simply correct and that's it. They don't have the capacity or the self-confidence to take 10 seconds and think, "What if I were wrong, how would that be?"

It takes a big man to freely admit that he is wrong. It takes a special kind of big dumb fuck to hold steadfast to being right when the entire world hates you for a reason.

The chances of a problem you're having actually being the fault of everyone else are so slim that they make Calista Flockhart look like the lead singer of Heart.

I promise, 98% of the time that instinctual tendency to look introspectively first will not backfire. Not to mention, as a parent, you look like a giant asswipe for not curbing that behavior when they were 4. A lot of people blame the parents. I blame both. I blame the parents while the children are young and the child once he/she grows up and should know better. If your child is freaking out in a grocery store, don't just stop them, explain that they shouldn't be ruining everyone else's shopping experience because Mommy and Daddy are pussies and don't know how to explain to their "precious little one" that the world doesn't care about them unless they grow up to make some money or be hot enough to marry someone who does.

In conclusion, parents generally suck and their children suck by genetics. Stop the cycle of moronism now while it is still possible. Teach your child that you can have them committed anytime you like and the world will simply continue to spin. Teach your children that they could be whining away in a padded room wearing a strait jacket and the school bus will still come the next day to pick up everyone else's children who didn't get put away because they weren't annoying. Merry Christmas and Happy Holidays!

Lesson 15:

If you are too selfish to spend the time creating a human being that will enrich the lives of others and contribute to the world, perhaps you shouldn't create a child. I have said it before and I will say it again. I am too selfish to have kids. If the time arrives when I feel I am no longer this way, I would love to usher a child into the world. Until then, I view it as a selfless act to wait until I am selfless enough to devote the proper attention to raising them before allowing them to spring forth from my groin. Speaking of groins...

Part 2:
"Like being kicked in the balls real slow."

I sometimes wonder if there a sign on my forehead that reads, "I live to make you happy. Please ask anything of me and disregard that I may have an existence outside of when you lay eyes on me." Aside from the fact that, if there is, my forehead is far larger than I had previously realized, this also would explain the interactions I have with many people.

Lately, I have been realizing that people assume that once I walk away from them, I simply stop existing until they need something from me again. Like when the credits role during a movie after you watched the main characters laughing and speaking inaudibly at the dinner table. That is all nice and good; but, what people need to realize is that after the credits have rolled and they have left the theater, those characters have to clean up the dishes, get ready for bed, get in a small argument about who emptied the dishwasher last and then fall asleep under a cloud of slightly uncomfortable silence because one of those lazy bastards isn't pulling their weight around there.

Things continue after we stop observing them. While yes, I agreed to do something, I have a life outside of this favor to which I have bound myself. I recently agreed to do a local play. [I used to have dreams of being a professional actor. Now, I just dream of getting good reviews in the Penny Saver. But I digress.] When the director asked me to be at rehearsal early after he has wasted countless hours of my life by being disorganized and having me be at every rehearsal when I was needed for none, and then asks me to come early so he can play catch-up, he assumed that I stopped existing after that role of credits (It's a metaphor). He is assuming, until the sequel comes out, I am simply freeze-framed and left smiling at that stupid fucking dinner table. Well, I am not! I am cleaning, arguing, sleeping and working when he is not around me. I am scrambling to make time for him to waste. Why? I have no idea.

Unfortunately it's not just him. It's people at work, people on the street and just every narcissistic bastard I come across nowadays. In short, it makes my (granted I try to keep interaction to a minimum) interaction with people like "getting kicked in the balls real slow" as a friend of mine so eloquently put it once. I have to stop here and point out the irony in that the person who coined this phrase was one of the biggest offenders of this kind of selfishness. We no longer speak.

Lesson 16:
We need to realize that there are lives attached to the people from whom we are "only asking for a couple hours". Realize that any minute received from them, they are taking from themselves to give away and for this, the person asking for this time should be grateful.

Speaking of being kicked in the balls, I haven't talked about my job much...

Part 3:
"I'm not a proctologist; but I'm fairly certain you are an asshole."

I have been thinking a lot lately about work and the people I have encountered as I fumbl around figuring out what I want to be when I grew up.

I used to conduct background investigations for a living and part of my job was to type up reports that were subsequently reviewed by moderately intelligent chimpanzees. Normally I wouldn't mind this; however, after a year or two, it began to become rather taxing because my voicemail can't handle the influx of messages from the third chimpanzee on the right basically making it very clear that I knew how to do their job better than they did.

Granted, they would never admit this, even when I politely point out that what they were saying was incorrect. Instead, they simply adjusted slightly what they were saying so that the changes I "needed" to make were a matter of opinion, which allowed them to keep from having to admit they are wrong.

I am sure that everyone encounters people like this. But, the lengths to which these circus primates would go in order to not admit to themselves that they were not qualified for anything more complicated than running the tilta-whirl at Six Flags America was incredible. Please, allow me to provide an example. No, really. You took the time to buy the book. The least I can do is flesh it out a little.

For example, if I had written,

"The Subject and Jones met through work in 02/2000 and have since had weekly social contact for dinners, movies and conversation."

I might have been sent a message that asks what their social contact consisted of. When I would point out that the information is, in fact, in the report and reading the report at all might cut down on this kind of mistake, I might expect the following message.

"It might be better to write this, 'The Subject first met Jones in 02/2000 when the Subject first came to work and they have met for dinners, movies and conversation once a week until present.' Please make these changes and resubmit the case."

This was almost word for word the editing suggestion I received. We can skip over the fact that it was reworded into an awkward sentence.

It seems as though my "career", as it stands, is just a montage of inept people taking down to me while I yawn. I don't expect to take the world by storm or have them see any value in me as I run out the door at exactly 5pm and not a minute after; but, would it be too much to ask to have the stupidity hidden? Can they pretend to have things under control so that it doesn't feel like I'm being lectured on public appearance by Britney Spears?

Lesson 17:

As a cynic, you are going to encounter a lot of people who just suck. They might suck at life, at work, in bed, in the kitchen, hell some people might even suck at sucking. But, if you encounter those that suck, don't expect them to act as though they do not suck. Just count to ten, take a deep breath, and smile. The cynic is growing inside of you and, while your change in expectations won't make them suck less, it might make your day do so to a small extent.

Speaking of sucking a little...

Part 4:
"I Gave Her My Heart and She Gave Me a Pen."

John Cusack says the above quote in the movie "Say Anything." It is a movie everyone has seen. Every chick loves it. Every dude secretly loves it and pretends not to. This movie always comes to my mind not when I begin a relationship, but, when I end one. I recently ended yet another failed attempt at a relationship. I had facts to back up every complaint. I had responses to knock down every bullshit attempt at a defense. I felt validated and secure regarding the manner in which I had stood up for myself.

What am I again left with? My dignity...and a pen. Sure, I defended my integrity and this time I didn't allow someone else to dictate how I felt about myself. [Granted, even when I allow that to happen it usually lasts about half a day.] But, I can't help but wonder, (what a lazy transition. I sound like Carry Bradshaw...and just like that every straight dude that bought this book just closed it) is everyone selfish but me?

If someone I have affection for says I am mistreating them, the first thing I do is question myself. I stop, step back and examine the possibility that it might be true.

"Wait, am I the asshole here?" I might ask myself.

"No, no...I'm fine." I usually answer.

But, I still take the time to wonder. I don't ever take the chance that someone I care for might be made to feel negatively at my hand. Why is this such a rare act?

It should be the very basest of considerations. Being wrong is not the end of the world. It is a prerequisite for being human. The un-hesitant admittance of which is something I take pride.

I am certain that I will know the love of my life. This person will be tough as I am but able to curb me when I need it. More importantly, they will back down and concede when the alternative is I believe them not to care. They will be wrong with confidence; because, it isn't the end of the world. It is the weakest of the human race that rally against being wrong as if their very nature were being threatened. Anyone who would lay the undue blame on a loved one because they don't want the inconvenience of introspection lacks integrity, plain and simple.

I will know the love of my life because they will do things wrong. Then they will apologize, commit to a change and own the bumps in their progress as much as they own their achievements. The love of my life will ask themselves, "Am I the asshole here?" And even if the answer turns out to be "No, no...I'm fine." They will then look for ways the miscommunication happened. They won't rush to throw it in the face of those they claim to respect. The love of my life won't make me say to myself, "I gave them the truth and they gave me a dial tone."

Lesson 18:

Be careful not to make someone a priority who is not willing to do the same. No matter how down we can feel and against ourselves we may be, we are all worth something. If that worth is not being realized by someone, it is just time to move on. It may be sad. It may feel unfinished. But, when you do it, you are proving to yourself you are worth more than the other person was determined not to realize. I find that helping to dig the ever expanding chasm of cynicism is a shovel made of other people's bullshit.

Speaking of shovels...

Part 5:

"Sir, I realize my left eye just fell out. I'll handle it. Just get the paperwork ready for the sale of the car."

I have been cynical almost my entire life. So much so, that I have lost almost all panic response. When you expect the worst, anything less than the worst is a happy surprise. As a child, I once used a shovel to bash the shit out of a landscape light next to a walkway at my childhood home. I remember doing it. I also remember not having any reason for it. It had a chip in it and, for some reason, that meant it was already broken and I was free to destroy the fuck out of this defenseless illuminating device. I just bashed the shit out of it until a spark flew and, from inside the house, my father yelled, "What the hell?"

Apparently, my little "game" had blown a fuse. My father is a patient and kind man. He is also not stupid and was a Special Agent with the FBI. Therefore, having witnessed me playing with a shovel near an electrical unit not 10 minutes before, wasted no time locating the scene of the crime.

Another child might have run before anyone found him holding the murder weapon. But, lacking a panic response and really not having any malice in my intent, I just sat and waiting for my dad to find me.

"Why the hell did you do that?" He asked, rightfully so. I really didn't have an answer and didn't see a point in wasting both of our time trying to think of some dumbass kid excuse like, "I didn't know that would happen." Lacking any better retort, I simply shrugged.

My father, as any normal human being would, wondered for a second if I might suddenly be slow witted. He took the shovel and looked at me, still expecting that I might pull together some stupid reason for doing what I had done. Knowing me and knowing that the chances for a lesson to be learned here had long since set sail, he simply said, "Quit doing things like this, Randy." This was sound advice. The problem in this situation was that I heard, "Stop hitting electrical devices with shovels." And to his credit, I never did hit another light with a shovel.

Because my luck has been so bad for so long, I am no longer surprised when things happen that are so bad that other people would panic. Just the other day I was cooking at my stove and my sister opened a bottle of champagne. [We weren't celebrating anything. We just like to act like we have money.] The cork flew off the bottle, rocketed across the room and missed my face by about 3 centimeters. Upon witnessing my lack of reaction, my sister exclaimed to one of her guests, "See? He has no panic response. Randy, tell them about how you lit your hand on fire." I then relayed the following story.

In my mid-twenties, I worked for a company with a couple of my friends. It was one of the few work environments I have enjoyed and when the company asked us all to work overtime to finish a project, I decided I would do it. I did not do this because I had suddenly grown some kind of work ethic. I did it because people I enjoyed being around would be there and I had no dog or boyfriend at the time and hence nothing better to do.

Realizing I would be at work rather late, I decided to break a personal rule and went to Wendy's and order a meal. I took it back to the office and got so busy, I was unable to eat it. About two hours later, I found time to eat and through the entire bag into the microwave and hit start. Bear in mind that I almost never eat fast food and even less frequently eat Wendy's. Had I frequented this establishment more often, I might have known that they wrap their burgers in tin foil and this would explain why the bag I had just placed in the microwave was smoking.

Hoping to keep the situation under wraps, I opened the door to the microwave and, with cat-like precision, retrieved the bag of smoking fast food from the microwave. Unfortunately, this simply served to rapidly oxygenate the smoldering inferno and the bag burst into flames in my hand. Upon witnessing my self-immolation, a couple of the ladies who had been waiting for their turn at the microwave let out a collective shriek. I calmly placed the bag in the sink, turned on the water and went to see what was in the vending machines.

Later, a friend of mine asked why I had no response to my hand suddenly pulling a Richard Pryer impression. My response was,

"Really, Kat? At this point, is it that surprising?"

She laughed uncomfortably, realizing I was right. Her mind undoubtedly had rocketed to the memory of the day before when she, our mutual friend and I went out for lunch. On our way back, I was sitting in the back seat when, without warning, my door opened and had it not been for my seatbelt, I would have simply crumbled underneath the rear wheel of our vehicle. I simple redistributed my weight and closed the door. Kat turned from the front seat and asked with concern, "Did you just almost fall out of the car?" Without looking up from my phone, on which I had been playing a game, I responded with genuine apathy, "Yes, Kat. Yes, I did."

In my twenties, I was restless. I frequently wanted to move around the furniture in my room, rearrange the kitchen and I frequently wanted to change vehicles. None of these things were asking a particularly large amount from me. However, the problem is, I went about these things rather impulsively. I was at work one day and decided I wanted a new car. I went on the internet and found that Enterprise Rental sold their old rentals for good prices and you could trade in your vehicle.

I decided I would go wash my car at lunch and take it to Enterprise to see what they might offer me. The car I drove at the time had a non-retractable antennae protruding from the hood. Remember this, it will be important soon. I only had an hour for lunch and I have to admit that I was in a little bit of a rush.

I arrived at the self-service car wash and hurriedly inserted a couple dollars and began scrubbing my car with the foam brush. In my haste, I failed to realize that I had bent the non-retractable (yet very sturdy) antennae down against the hood of the car. As I leaned forward, pushing the brush along the hood of my car, the antennae suddenly, having had enough of being bent to its brink, rocketed back towards me and hit me directly in my left eye.

I have to interject here and point out that I had always found it stupid when people screamed in movies when they were hurt. I am not speaking of the times when someone is gravely injured; but, when someone is injured in a slap-stick fashion in a movie and let out that whale that is clearly intended to illicit a cheap laugh from the audience, I always found it to be a stretch. It isn't.

Once the antennae hit me in the eye I suddenly found myself against the back wall of the car wash. My body and mind had been ill prepared for the literal assault on my senses and hence had not taken the standard deep breath. I found myself unable to breathe for a second and then taking the biggest breath I had ever taken to date. I then experience a fascinating phenomenon. I let out this visceral and primal scream that echoed through the brick-lined walls of the car wash.

After staggering back and for a while, I realized that I could not see out of my left eye. It wasn't black like it is in the movies. On the contrary, it was like I was trying to see the world through a full glass of whole milk. A slew of other car wash patrons came to my rescue in order to make sure I wasn't being murdered. This situation was made even more awkward by the fact that by the time they arrived, the antennae had stopped wiggling back and forth and it appeared that I just simply decided I was sick and tired of washing my car, had flung myself against the wall and begun to scream. I waved them off and pointed to my eye as if to say, "I am not crazy! But, go away I have to finish washing my car even though I may be blind now."

I rinsed off my car quickly and found myself to be very angry. Not scared, not worried, I was very angry. Why couldn't I just get my car washed? Why was it asking too much of the gods to simply let me rush and get something done? I decided that I was not going to be deterred. I called my mother and left her a voicemail saying that I would be in the emergency room because I had injured my eye; but first, I was going to go to Enterprise Rental Car. This, in my mind, seemed self-explanatory.

I arrived at Enterprise and I could see the eyelashes of my left eye by using my right eye. I could still open it enough to expose the blood red part of my eye that used to be white. I was sweating rather profusely from the adrenaline rush and was so angry that I really didn't have the patience to explain anything except why I was there.

I am fairly certain the lady at the front desk simply thought I was deformed and ignored my left eye. I appreciated this. I explained my purpose for being there and was led back to a salesperson that, upon looking at me, let out an audible, "Wha!"

I advised the gentleman that I had injured my eye earlier and would be seeking medical treatment; however, before I did that, I wanted to have him give me an estimate of what I might get for my car. He seemed perplexed. I had no patience for this. He asked if I needed an ambulance and I responded that I simply needed an estimate. The estimate wasn't high enough to warrant me trading in my car. I felt this was the proper time to go to the ER.

By the time I saw the doctor, the swelling had gone down considerably. However, the vision in my left eye still resembled milk; although by this time, 2% milk. He informed me that the corneal abrasion would fix itself but that my left eye was drooping slightly and this caused him some concern. I asked to go to the bathroom and quickly removed the eye patch he had so carefully placed over my left eye. My physical insecurity swelled to epic proportions as I realized, the drooping to which the doctor had been referring, was simply what my eye looked like before I ever sent a car antennae into it at 200mph. I re-taped my eye patch and went home in my old car.

Lesson 19:

You have to be able to laugh at yourself. Anyone can look at the above anecdotes and laugh years later. I laughed about them that day. Why? Because, in the end, crying about them wasn't going to make them any less painful. Laughing about them did. I joked about my bad luck. My friends poked fun and I went to bed knowing that I had endured yet again. It is hard to do the first couple times; but, it is a satisfying feeling to know that, whatever happens, you will laugh your way through it. It was a gift that got me through a large portion of my twenties. Speaking of my twenties...

Chapter 6
Part 1:
"Money makes the world go round. But, I used to do that."

As previously stated, in my twenties, I was restless. At around 26, I had been thinking a lot lately about how I had no money and was never really able to reassure myself that I would ever have any. I was fairly certain that I could classify myself as successful. I was 26, I owned my own business, I made a fairly good living and had beaucoup experience in pretty much every area of work including federal security. Now, here was the problem. I could have gotten hit by a bus at any moment!

I couldn't live for when I was 50 because, I might not make it that far. If I want a DVD, why couldn't I buy one? Now I realize I might have come off as somewhat selfish; but, the thing is I really didn't care.

I didn't have any children, I was not married and I had no one depending on me but me. I had not had children because I was far from ready to not have my world revolve around anyone but me.

Don't get me wrong, I was not that little kid who stayed home sick and was shocked that the school bus still made its rounds despite the fact that I was not going to school; however, I must say that I was the kind of adult who wanted things the way young children want toys.

I was not irresponsible. I was, for the most part, financially independent. If I want to treat myself to a DVD of season two of the Golden Girls to keep me from running a hot bath and frantically searching for a razor, then hey, that's what I was going to do. I did not live an extravagant life. I did not spend money on myself ever. I was poor. I did not have a lot of money and I was trying hard to get to the point where I was not looking in the couch for quarters and trying to find CD's I can sell back in order to pay my $25 dollar credit card bill cause I just bought season two of the Golden Girls.

I wanted money and I wished living life in a good way didn't depend on it so much; but, I felt the small twinge of happiness hidden in the fact that I could purchase for myself small things that would never amount to a retirement fund that will support me when I am shiny on top. My father used to tell me, "You may have to be unhappy for 3 months in order to be happy for years to come." This is truly good advice, it really is. But, all I could think was, "But, what if I get hit by a bus tomorrow? I'll be pissed."

I vowed that I would find a happy medium between being responsible and happy. I would spend money but also save it. I would make myself happy while still protecting my future self. I didn't.

Rapidly approaching my mid-thirties and my aforementioned business has failed, I bought a house just before the bubble burst, I went deep into debt making it livable and I have officially borrowed more money from my sister in the past year than I collectively borrowed from anyone my entire life. But, it's the thought that counts. And I'm thinking I still might want to hold off on children.

Lesson 20:

Be careful not to complain about blessings. This seems obvious. However, you would be surprised how much you might be prone to doing this. My greatest example is how often I complain about being in a position where I have to borrow money from my sister. Yes, she always gets it back. Yes, she loans it to me with no pretense or resentment. But, I hate that I have to borrow it in the first place and I frequently find myself complaining about it. Then I kick myself for not being grateful for having the kind of support I have and having the ability to borrow money when the need arises. There are many in the world without that luxury and I should remember that more. While on the subject of my sister...

Part 2:

"I just checked 'plus one' on your wedding invite because I am bringing a bottle of Grey Goose."

Driving home from a family function recently, my sister decided to have an impromptu intervention regarding my drinking. Well, it was more about me passing out all the time, but, potato/potato. [That doesn't translate so well in text.]

Bear in mind this was coming from a girl who, during a childhood fight, scratched a mole off of my neck, flicked it at me and yelled, "Now you are gonna get cancer!" All that aside, she seemed genuinely concerned.

It wasn't so much that she was genuinely concerned about me being an alcoholic. It was more that I was so unabashed about drinking to the point where I needed a nap during a party where my parents were in attendance. I feel the need to shed some light on the fact that by the time I hit 30 I had developed a well-deserved reputation for being "the rally-er". I could drink with the best of them, lay down for 20 minutes and then rally for the rest of the night just fine.

I developed this skill because I never really drank before I was 28. My first real relationship lasted almost my entire twenties and, when it ended abruptly, I realized that when I drank, I thought less. Up until then, I never liked that it just made me tired. But, once I started drinking, I didn't want to miss out on things just because I was sleepy. So, I developed my napping ability. I am in no way implying that drinking in order to deal with anything is healthy. It is just how I chose/choose to handle little things in my life that demand a lot of attention but deserve little.

During the intervention, I relayed that it wasn't that I was unhappy. I was just bored. In a situation where I know I am not driving and I am loved unconditionally by those around me, why shouldn't I drink till I fell asleep? The look on her face and the lack of response was all the rebuttal I needed. I knew what I was doing wasn't permanent. I knew I just wasn't where I wanted to be in my life. What we have learned about being a cynic so far is that it isn't about being unhappy. It is about realizing that unhappiness is temporary and we need to make fun of it while it's around.

Regardless, I appreciated the concern my sister showed by having this talk with me and decided I would reserve drinking for the weekends. Subsequently, the passages that you found less entertaining here were most likely written on a week day.

I had alcoholics in my family and I knew my behavior was not alcoholism. I also knew I was being lazy. I could go home and write. I could carry around a pen and paper and make notes about things to write later. (...like I want to be one of those assholes). The point being, I knew I wasn't being the person I was always going to be. At 33, I was still a fucking child in many ways and this pissed me off. It was particularly biting since I held a sense of pure superiority over most of the world's populace.

The real problem waiting in the wings was that many of my friends were moving forward with their lives and I was feeling stagnant. I hated my job. I was perpetually single and mostly it was my fault. My best friend had recently gotten engaged and I felt none of the cliché jealously or angst towards her. I felt nothing but happiness for her. However, I did feel less than happy about having to find a date to the wedding. I am not the luckiest guy in love and the point that would need to be reached in a relationship in order for me to invite him to a wedding was just too much work for me at this point.

That night I dreamed of just bringing a bottle of Grey Goose to the wedding. We wouldn't need to speak. During the particularly touching parts of the wedding, I would look over and wink suggestively. I would know that we were temporary. But, the romantic nature of the moment would encourage me to keep up the façade for the night. Maybe, every once in a while, I would reach over and gently wipe the perspiration from GG's face. Towards the end of the night, as the bride and groom made their way to their honeymoon, I would look over at him, half-empty and say, "Thanks for coming." What a night. The dancing would probably get a little awkward.

Lesson 21:
Sometimes, shit just happens and there is no lesson to learn. You will from time to time find yourself in a bad place. As long as you know you won't be there forever and you keep your eye on the prize, it is sometimes necessary to just go with it. Sometimes, you just have to own your bad

place and dance the awkward dance with your vodka date with pride. Speaking of awkward...

Part 3:

"Staples hold up remarkably well in the washing machine."

As a child I went to catholic school for a time. Should I have capitalized *catholic?* Who cares? Anyway, the things that stick out in my brain are not the teachings of heaven and hell and how to get to each place respectively. But, what stand out are the really pedantic things the faculty concerned themselves with in the absence of actual facts to teach.

I recall during my second grade year, the hem fell out of my uniform pants and my father was called from his office. Bear in mind here, my father worked at the FBI in Washington, DC, the annoying traffic capitol of the world and my school was in a suburb a good 40 minute drive away.

Even as a 7 year old, I sat in the front office looking at these people like they were crazy. Was I really missing class because my hem fell out? Seriously? That having been said, my inner monologue frequently expressed itself with more confidence than my outward demeanor. I am sure I was crying. He arrived less than happy that a wardrobe malfunction had caused him to miss half a day's worth of work, as if he wasn't already concerned enough I would turn out gay (he's fine with it now). My father pulled me over to the secretary's desk, wiped my eyes and promptly stapled my hem back in place with a stapler he had commandeered from the secretary without asking.

I frequently use this as an example of how confident my father is. I love that he just doesn't understand embarrassment. I remember exactly how he looked at me, as if to say, "What? What's the problem? Why are you crying? It's fixed."

Looking back, I am rather proud of him for making this situation embarrassing for the faculty. What an easy fix that could have been implemented by any one of the countless adults I had been surrounded by while my father made his way to me. I understand entirely now why he didn't understand that the situation was embarrassing to me. I was a rather annoyingly fragile child and I was humiliated that I would have staples hanging off of my pants the rest of the day. I could only imagine the ridicule. "Look, he is too poor for thread!"

The reason this moment sticks out in my memory is not because it bothered me. It is because my father set an example for me without even trying to. It just goes to show you that "traumatic" moments in life can pave the way for all the right coping mechanisms for a cynic. As I sit here writing this at work, while I should be earning the paycheck they so reluctantly deposit in my account every two weeks, I am noticing that the right leg of pants is hemmed with several staples. I had forgotten that I had done this. I remember exactly when my hem fell out. It was two years ago.

Lesson 22:
The moments that haunt you from childhood can be your biggest strengths. Let no horrible situation go unused. Let no clumsy fall go un-laughed at. Reach back to the embarrassing memory and use it to your own advantage. Let no hem go unstapled. On the subject of embarrassing moments...

Part 4:
"They found him suffocated under 1 ton of toilet paper at the end of the stalls."

I am going to begin this anecdote by telling you that it contains way too much information about me. I must unavoidably tell you that I suffer from Irritable Bowel Syndrome. I find no shame in this; however, it is not something I like to discuss at the drop of a hat.

However, when it comes to being a cynic, one must learn to emerge from embarrassing moments with an ill-earned sense of honor. I wish that my embarrassing moments were birthed solely from my aforementioned intestinal trouble. Alas, my humility knows no bounds. But let's face it. The poo stories tend to be the funnier ones.

I used to drive to New York City a lot to visit a friend and along the way I made friends with quite a few rest stops. I remember a particularly memorable encounter where I barely made it into a stall at the end of line. While the sheer urgency of the situation might burn this into one's memory, what really makes it stand out is the state the bathroom was in before I ever reached it.

As I sprinted in, I noticed that the floor was wet. Luckily, I only lost my footing for a few seconds and sort of wind surfed into the stall. As I sat, minding my own business, I noticed that there was a large industrial strength dryer undoubtedly put there to fix the wet floor situation. As I write this, I struggle to impress upon you the strength with which this dryer was emitting air.

To put it into prospective, every time I tore a section of toilet paper off of the roll, I watched as it was swept up in the cyclone of warm sewer air and carried beneath the edge of the stall in which I sat to an unknown location. In truly stupid fashion, I attempted this several times before realized that I had to pull with one hand, pin the top of the toilet paper section to the stall and, with my other hand, rip it from the roll. I then had to hold it very carefully above my head while folding it to keep it out of reach of the gale force winds stripping the hair from my legs.

As I was wrapping things up as it were, I washed my hands and surfed on the sole of my shoes out of the wet bathroom. On my way out, I caught a glimpse of something truly fascinating to me. Underneath the door of the last stall opposite from where I had been doing what needed to be done, I spotted a pair of legs. Surrounding this poor man's appendages were pounds of toilet paper. This was absolutely the same toilet paper I had attempted to tear from the role and that had been swiftly stolen from me from the industrial hurricane at the other end of the room.

The paper had been carried through 5 stalls and had all culminated at the end. As I hastily made my way back to my car, I wondered what kind of man he must have been. "Why not say something?" I thought to myself. But, logic getting the better of me, my thought process changed. What would he say? "Hey, where the fuck is all this toilet paper coming from?"

Had the toilet paper been blown from an empty stall and other bathroom users were to hear him express wonder at the place from which the toilet paper was originating, they might find him strange. That having been said, if he imagined it was just some asshole flinging toilet paper into his cell, what kept him from saying anything? Did he believe himself to be a subject of very odd bullying? Had this happened before and this man had spent so much time in bathrooms with cartoon wind machines that he was no longer flappable by such amateur agitation.

Regardless, I still look back at this man's legs. I still wonder if maybe he was just asleep (as if that would be there weirdest thing I have ever seen in a Jersey rest stop).

Lesson 23:

Sometimes, you just have to roll with punches. You simply have to be grateful for the little things. Despite the fact that my genetics had cursed me with a horrible digestive system, I was grateful I got to the toilet in time. Maybe that man was grateful for the same thing and didn't have it in him to complain about toilet paper being blown into his stall. Maybe it wasn't shocking to him that this was happening because he had luck that was similar to mine. Maybe he was engrossed in the situation at hand and just didn't give a shit about anything else. Pun intended. That having been said, it was a New Jersey rest stop. Maybe he was just glad it was toilet paper and not syringes. Now *that's* a cynic.

Speaking of shit storms...

Part 5:
"The Faux Bi-Polar Text Carpet Bomb."

Our final anecdote finds us on a homosexual date (Shocking). Obviously the names have been changed in order to avoid being sued. Dude 1 (me) and dude 2 (this douche bag named Tony) met in a bar. Not the least cliché thing to ever happen but it trumps online which is usually how everyone meets nowadays in the gayborhood. I got his number and we made a plan to have dinner. This was confirmed by a text by me which read, "Call me tomorrow to confirm." I received an affirmative response on his part. I never received the follow-up phone call. You may be thinking this is where I get disappointed. It isn't. I forgot totally about it because I expected him to be a douche. I ran into Tony about a month later in the same bar and he was upset that we never had dinner. I explained he was supposed to confirm and we agreed that it was just a miscommunication and we would continue on.

We had a reasonably nice time together at the bar; but, Tony kept periodically glaring at me and telling people to stop talking to me. I eventually found out that he had been very drunk when he arrived and kept forgetting that we had established that we had a miscommunication previously. He would go on to spend another hour or so going back and forth between talking about our upcoming dinner and then being angry and glaring at me and storming out. Now many people would be turned off at this point. I, being the understanding and non-judgmental man I am, realized that I am no stranger to the devil's nectar and decided not to hold it against him. I texted him that it bugged me that he left and that I liked him but if he was like this sober, I was out. The next day, after I reminded him of most of the behavior from the previous night and me being very understanding, we made dinner plans for the following night.

I should interject that I was incredibly emotionally bored during this time in my life. It was one of those phases that you can tell you are in but cannot do anything about it. I was starving for romantic interaction, even if it wasn't terribly positive. I was so very immensely bored.

Tony and I had our first date at my house. I cooked dinner and gave him a tour of my lovely home that ended on my roof-top deck overlooking the harbor and the city. The date lasted about 5 hours and we kissed. During the date, we discussed several topics, laughed a lot and he opened up to me about his ex of 6 years being bi-polar (remember this for later, it's important).

I was floored by how much I enjoyed his company. I was terribly excited to see him again and so relieved he wasn't displaying so many of the traits I had come to expect from the queers I had previously had the displeasure of encountering. I walked him to his car and he gave me one last kiss and told me he would text me when he got home. He didn't. The next day, I texted him with, "I assume you made it home alive." The response I got was, "Yeah, sorry. I just hopped right into bed." Being still high from the previous night's surprisingly enjoyable date, I decided to be nice. "I had a really good time last night." And here, gentle readers, is where disappointment begins to peak out from behind the pleasant surprise. He wrote, "Same."

I gave it a few hours and pretended to give a shit at work and then wrote something else to him to subtly prompt him to ask me out again. I got no response. I waited a couple more hours and then decided that I had been really understanding of his behavior the first night we interacted and that maybe I had some wiggle room. I then texted him, "Hey, you are probably busy. But, clearly I will have to take charge and ask if you want to have drinks on Friday. ;-)" I got the response "cool". I am not perfect and I will admit that one of my flaws is a lack of understanding of why someone would continue to agree to date (however unenthusiastically they do it) if they weren't interested. I have never had a problem being completely honest. It is because of this that I frequently miss the clues. My thinking being, they would simply tell me. Additionally, I normally would not have been putting anywhere near this much effort in. Remember, I was so very bored. However, let's head back to the pleasant surprise theory of disappointment.

I had been so surprised by the good time and potential for future good times, I was somewhat blinded to the lackluster response I was getting. To be fair to him, this could have just been the way he was at work. He could have just been busy. He could just not communicate well over text. The previously mentioned over-communication that I was exhibiting was not helpful. I will admit this.

That having been said, I called him the next day to make sure that "cool" meant we actually had a date for Friday. He informed me that he thought he had responded and eventually mentioned that he thought I was being rather sensitive and it was "a lot to take from someone he had just met." My mind immediately shot to the first time we had spent time together and, after an hour of knowing me, he had glared, been possessive, referred to me as his "baby" and stormed out in a fit. Not that these were indicators of actual feelings; but, I thought that maybe he might avoid flattering himself with whatever conclusions he had been drawing from my behavior. You know, like I had done for him. We established that we would see each other that Friday and I got off the phone feeling as though I had been acting like one of those chicks that imagines weddings after the first date. I knew I hadn't been; but, Tony was manipulating it to seem that way so that he could get some ego stroking. Or at least that is the narcissistic theory I have formed in order to sleep at night. Either way, the story continues.

Two days later, on Thursday, I texted him to ask if he would like me to come to him for our drinks the next day or if he would to come to me. I got no response. That night, I texted one last time, asking him to let me know by the morning. I got nothing. The next day (the day we were supposed to have our date), I texted him to let me know about that night and, several hours later, received "I think I need to cancel...". Being a man of thick skin and unmatched stubbornness, I called him. The following is a transcript of the conversation.

Tony: Hello?

Randy: Hey. So, what's up now?

Tony: I have to cancel. I went to a happy hour and I'm here now. But, I'll call you later.

Randy: Ugh, bye.

Not surprisingly, he never called. My logic in being angry here is that is so disrespectful to cancel on someone last minute after ignoring their attempts to solidify plans. It is also even worse to inform them you are canceling because you decided to do something else on a whim. It was at this point that I felt as though I had been tricked into making him feel better about himself for a short period of time and now he was bored. I decided I was not comfortable with this. What follows may be difficult to stomach...for you. I'm fine with it.

I then decided to abandon all hopes of anything with Tony and, along with that, any concern for his view of me or my behavior. It was then that I decided I wanted to feel better about the situation. I remembered that he had dealt before with bi-polar drama and that I would see what his threshold for misery might be. What? I was just curious.

I started by texting him the following day that I would like to be friends. I then waited a day and texted him that if he was going to ignore me I wouldn't be friends with him. I then texted him the next day as if I hadn't texted him any of the other texts. It was something like, "Hey, how is your day?" Then I waited 2 days and wrote a mixture of the two, "You still owe me a drink and for ignoring my texts." I then got a confusing response, "Not ignoring, just been really busy."

This threw a monkey wrench in my game. What the fuck did that mean? Was he still trying to date? Why would he clearly ignore me for 4 days and then suddenly want to dispel that appearance of apathy? Why would he ignore my attempts at friendship, fake as they may have been, and then want me to know he wasn't ignoring me? This was fascinating. Tony was a more formidable opponent than I had realized.

I have to admit here, I thought about trying to salvage something. "Maybe it's not too late." I thought. But then came another day of ignoring my texts. He had done it to me again. He had seen me attempting to toy with him and he turned the tables. He got to me! This was unacceptable.

He had manipulated me into stroking his ego twice and I got nothing out of it. I then spent the next couple of days bombarding his phone with text ranging such a wide spectrum that it frequently made me giggle when I hit send.

"I'm sorry I fucked things up."

"What is your problem?"

"I thought you said we went to the same middle school, how come you aren't in my year book?"

"I couldn't tell you were serious. I'm really sorry."

This goes on and on, while I made sure that no text held the same emotional content. See what I did there? Played on the one thing I knew he would subconsciously be bugged by, the faux bi-polar text carpet bomb. The last I heard from Tony was a simple, "Please stop texting me." I smiled a little when I read it. I then kind of felt bad and damn it if I still wasn't a little disappointed that such potential had been wiped out.

You may be thinking to yourself, "That is emotional terrorism. That was just a way to placate, at all costs, an adolescent need for superiority by acting in a ridiculous and mentally insensitive manner." And you would be correct.

Lesson 24:

Love will make you do very stupid things. The pursuit of love may make you lose your damn mind. It is imperative that you never lose sight of who you are. You will act like someone else. You will say things you don't mean. You may terrorize a poor man via text message simply because he did something he very well may not have even known he did. These little trips down insanity lane happen. But, you must return. You must get yourself back on the right path. The person for you may be on that path and if you are still on "I don't care what anyone thinks about me!" street, you might miss out on them. That would be a truly sad ending to the story of your life. Speaking of endings...

The Final Lesson:

Each and every one of us has a cynic inside. It isn't about being an optimist or a pessimist or even an atheist. Cynicism is about being. Life is going to be what it is. Try really hard to make yours what you want. This won't be in vain. But, during the times between when you feel like nothing is working, just accept it. Move on!

My uncle is an actor and he was in a movie with Dolly Parton, the name of which escapes me, in which she says, "Get down off the cross, honey. Somebody needs the wood." I find this to be wonderful advice for the cynic. Just say something funny. Short of that, think something funny. Short of that, do something funny. The point is, never forget that life is to be lived. And living is to be mocked whenever possible.

Whatever road brought you to where you are, just remember, there are some who can't make it down the road at all. It isn't about what brought you to where you are but where you are headed and what you do with this life.

My very favorite quote comes from somewhere I cannot recall. I have "interneted" and researched and tried hard to find the source. After exhausting all venues, I am forced to come to the conclusion that I made it up.

"Everyone is always so worried about whether the glass if half empty or half full. Me? I just drink what's in the glass."

ABOUT THE AUTHOR

Who the hell am I to be giving you advice? I am no one. But, I have learned a great deal in my short time on this earth. I don't pretend to say things that others do not know. But, I hope that my sense of humor and my observations can contribute to more than just a night at my house with my friends and some wine (although, that is pretty nice too). Randall W. Dunkle lives in Baltimore, MD and is in constant pursuit of happiness...or something like it.